Phil Goes Home for Christmas
Copyright © 2022 Burds of a Feather Publishing

All rights reserved. No part of this publication may be reproduced, distributed, or transmitted in any form or by any means, including photocopying, recording, or other electronic or mechanical methods, without the prior written permission of the publisher, except in the case of brief quotations embodied in critical reviews and certain other noncommercial uses permitted by copyright law. For permission requests, write to the publisher, addressed "Attention: Permissions Coordinator," at the address below.

Written by Trina Harris Cambrice
Illustrated by Jasmine Burds

Burds of a Feather Publishing
PO Box 750024
New Orleans, La. 70175

W: www.burdsofafeatherpublishing.com
E: info@burdsofafeatherpublishing.com

This book is dedicated to the new addition to my family- Legend Amir Harris.

Love,
Grandma

THIS BOOK BELONGS TO

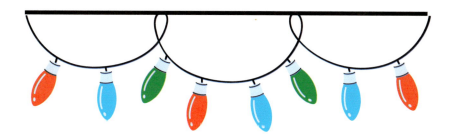

One winter morning, Phil and GiGi were sitting along the banks of the Mississippi River.
Out of nowhere Phil shouted to GiGi
"I want to visit my family for Christmas"!

"Where is your family?" GiGi replied.

"They are on the West Coast, in California", said Phil.

After boarding the plane, Phil looked around for GiGi. He spotted her flying on the side of the plane.

"What are you doing out there?", asked Phil.

"Flying" GiGi replied.

"But why aren't you on the plane?" said Phil.

"Because I have wings to fly", said GiGi.

Phil was so confused.

After a long flight, the plane finally landed.

GiGi waited outside for Phil to exit the plane.

"Here, I am" said Phil flapping his wings at Gigi.
"Fix your glasses", said Phil.

Ignoring Phil, GiGi walked to the beach. "It's so different, but so beautiful out here" she said, while looking at the Golden Gate Bridge.

"Of course it's beautiful, but it would look better if your glasses weren't upside down" Phil said while laughing hysterically.

Here comes Phil's dad, Mr. Fred.
He wore a monocle and a large pair of riding boots.

"Well, howdy Doody! We miss you little fellow" he said.

Phil looked so happy with a big smile on his face. His dad was a big pelican with fluffy brown and white feathers. He wobbled when he walked.

"Come on you guys. Let's meet the family",
his dad said.

As Phil and GiGi made their way to the beach, Phil's family and friends welcomed them with warm hugs.

As night began to fall, everyone gathered next to the campfire and started singing Christmas carols.

GiGi noticed that there were Pelicans of all colors joining in to sing with them.

"Wow! Are these all members of your family?" GiGi asked. "Yes" replied Phil. We are a family of many colors! With a proud look on face. He stood there for a moment overwhelmed with joy.

As the sun began to set, Phil and Gigi realized that it doesn't matter what color you are because families come in all colors!

Phil Goes Home for Christmas

Directions: Color Phil. Don't forget to draw his Christmas Hat!

Phil Goes Home For Christmas

Word Search

```
E C Q U Q D C V B D P R U V U
U M A B Q G K S R Q Z L G M X
X D R L T U R E M C G B A Z W
F L V I I F M W Z Z E G M N F
A E P G W F J S X Z A X B X E
U P A I R G O V N L V F Z P Q
C P J G X O R R Z C O R D E F
Y H K I S U L S N E E G J L B
R O J N W J I W Y I M O H I K
J P D S W E S T C O A S T C T
F C B B R I D G E W F P Q A U
T G Z F T S G R V G F V M N R
P K T D W N C H R I S T M A S
L V O B V M K Z H J R J Q M G
N G X W V M J J E V U P H I L
```

California	Christmas	West Coast	Phil
Pelican	Bridge	Plane	GiGi

Made in the USA
Columbia, SC
10 February 2025